Thoughts of Lost Man

Tears of the Forgotten Child

By Gary Clarke

Cadmus Publishing
CadmusPublishing.com

Thoughts of a Lost Man:
Tears of a Forgotten Child

Manufactured in the United States of America. Copyright 2025 by Gary Clarke. All rights reserved. No part of this book may be reproduced in any form, audio, digital, or in print, except excerpts by reviewers, without written permission from the copyright holder or Cadmus Publishing LLC.

DISCLAIMER:
The thoughts, opinions, and expressions herein are those of the author and do not reflect those of Cadmus Publishing LLC. Any similarities to actual events or people are purely coincidental. Names and distinguishing characteristics may have been changed to preserve the identities of any individuals. Published by Cadmus Publishing LLC. P. O. Box 8664. Haledon, NJ 07538

Web: Cadmuspublishing.com
Web: Booksbyprisoners.com
Web: MusicbyPrisoners.com
Facebook.com/Cadmuspublishing
Business email: admin@cadmuspublishing.com
Author email: info@cadmuspublishing.com
Phone: 360.565.6459

ISBN# 978-1-63751-518-1

Book Catalog Info Categories:
  Poetry

Cadmus Publishing
CadmusPublishing.com

Thoughts of a Lost Man—Gary Clarke

Dedication

I dedicate this book to four important women in my life. To my daughter Aniyah, you are a vital reason that I aspire to be a man that you deserve to call your father. You are the light that paves my way. To my mother Angie, you deserve to have a son that you are proud to claim and I work diligently every day to honor you. For my sister Shequita, the fact that you always look towards me for aid afforded me the ability to look within myself and grow to be reliable for you. To my love, my Queen Sh'mae, you came into my life and sheltered me with your love and grace and gave me a refuge so I can be comfortable being me. I thank you all.

For my brothers and sisters whose voices are muted or lack the ability to communicate your heartache, your pain, your depression, and your forgotten child just know that my eyes are your portal and my voice are your speakers. I see you, I hear you, I feel you and I am you. Console that child and you will find that adult and you shall start to feel harmony.

Thoughts of a Lost Man—Gary Clarke

Preface

Throughout the course of my life I've tried to discover why I had this aching sensation emanating from the core of my being. I often asked myself, "Why does it hurt so bad?" and "Why can't I fmd the source of this anguish?", yet I never found the solution. I used to look at my childhood pictures and rarely see myself smile, but those eyes, staring into those eyes... Those depressed eyes depicted a different scenario that I wasn't able to articulate. As I would look into those eyes the pain that I felt/feel would intensify and leave me immobilized. I was unaware if I was coming, going, or if I even existed.

I would lay back for countless hours on my bunk and search for the key to unlock this internal mystery. I started to write these poems as therapy and quickly discovered that it was the key that I've been seeking my whole life, yet when I opened the door all I heard was the sobbing of a young boy. I never saw the face of this child but his pain was evident as it usurped my physical composition. As I continued to write I figured out that I wasn't just writing poetry, but I was engaged in a conversation with the "Lost Man and Forgotten Child" and both never realized that they were in search of each other, they never knew that the other one even existed. Take a journey through the thoughts of a

Thoughts of a Lost Man—Gary Clarke

tormented soul searching for love, peace, redemption, freedom and acceptance.

Thoughts of a Lost Man—Gary Clarke

Table of Contents

Part #1

1. Lost Man Forgotten Child
2. Princess
3. Unforeseen Consequences
4. Reflection
5. Mental Battle of Self-Evolution
6. Paradoxical Freedom
7. Rotten' Nooses
8. Oblivious

Part #2

9. Lost Man Forgotten Child
10. Debilitating Realm
11. Grey's Anatomy
12. Lady Insanity Sings the Rage
13. What Was
14. Cocoon
15. Four Walls

Part #3

16. Lost Man Forgotten Child
17. First Love
18. A Letter to Mom
19. A Soul That Cries
20. 7 Years of Deprivation

Thoughts of a Lost Man—Gary Clarke

21.	A Precious Gift
22.	7 Years of Separation
23.	Limbo
24.	Solitude
25.	Solitary

Part #4

26.	Lost Man Forgotten Child
27.	I Fear no Tomorrows
28.	Beyond my Perception
29.	Beneath my Lenses I See Pain
30.	Ms. Direction
31.	Vent
32.	Humanity
33.	Love Outgrown

Part #5

34.	Lost Man Forgotten Child
35.	Contemplation
36.	Silence
37.	Lost Time
38.	Pain
39.	Lost Man Forgotten Child

Thoughts of a Lost Man—Gary Clarke

Lost Man Forgotten Child

    I'm submerged deep into the formlessness of my mind
    Captivated by atrocities, yet disoriented — Clueless
    Of what I'm in need in search of — What to find
    This vastness seems hollow, shallow but with each step
    I'm soaked, sinking deeper — I'm losing my concept of time
    Everything feels mysterious even though I'm familiar with the grime
    Comfortable with demise
    I feel at peace as I move through the whispers of sublime
    This moisture on my fingertips
    Reminds me of the pain I felt and couldn't distinguish it
    Muffled noises slip in my ears — Harmonize with emptiness, imprisonment
    I don't want to walk beyond this moment
    But this trench feels like it's limitless
    Echoes of drips wakes me to realize where I am
    Unconscious that I live in this

Thoughts of a Lost Man—Gary Clarke

Lost Man Forgotten Child Pt. I

My pain didn't begin with my incarceration — That anguish sparked with failed attempts

Of some form of emancipation

Young boy thinking he's a man - Yet -

The lack of guidance starved him   Remained in states of deprivation

Only option left   The streets   Sort of felt like an obligation

Struggling to juggle the two determined ideas

    Searching for justification

But I did more than feel pain   I inflicted it Confusion and sadness

New stages of gentrification

Weapons on one side/ Drugs on the other

While I'm stuck in the middle tears causing tsunamis on the pavement

Was my birthright to be a part of this modern day enslavement Or

Better options as a youth would've never left my mind so vacant

So I try to fit into the scheme   No longer having dreams

Because nobody ever encouraged that I can make it

Thoughts of a Lost Man—Gary Clarke

So I limited my steps / Smoked away my regrets

And pain was my dreams permanent replacement

Medication of the hood was used as a numbing agent

As the love drains and remains   Lost and locked away in the basement

Who could predict the decisions that an adolescent would be faced with

Those who came before me couldn't believe I was so strong - When my foundation was baseless

Objectives were nameless - Victims were faceless - Laugh while I'm in the face of danger

While internally I'm shaking

Counting the number of peers   Who lost fear

Now memorials are built on corners where their remains are left stinking

Grip up to defend / Pain is the best revenge Who has time for moral thinking

Tears increase the blinking

Mind disconnects from the eyes because visions of escaping causes internal bleeding

From depression that my spirit is constantly drinking

Neglecting the weight of pain with each step

I'm steadily sinking

Thoughts of a Lost Man—Gary Clarke

Princess

You are elegant and precious
A descendant from royalty
A princess
Be all that you choose to be
Best of the best   You are great
Never settle for anything less
Demand respect
Achieve the impossible   A princess will be a Queen Which you will evolve to be
A Queen runs her country   Inspires the world
You are more than just a girl
You are beautiful in everyway
Nobody in this world can get in your way
You are destined for greatness   God will pave the way
An angel is what you are A Queen is what you will be
You will always be my princess to me

Thoughts of a Lost Man—Gary Clarke

Unforeseen Consequences

Forever present yet rarely seen, Valuable but not always acknowledged

Precious, although to the unknown — worthless — Things taken for granted

Only appreciated once they're removed

Beautiful amongst a billion stars — Only visible when standing alone

An unforeseen consequence through well thought punishments

Life of bad decisions — Couldn't picture myself thinking from this position

Who know that you could be taken

When your existence exceeds generation to generation

These walls obstruct my vision Where my vision controls my mind

You begin to forget how you miss things — Until they reappear from a long period of time

The Sun, Clouds, and Stars are all visible to the naked eye

But the moon, I sit back and think and I want to cry

Thoughts of a Lost Man—Gary Clarke

    The last time I've seen you, it's been quiet sometime
    Nearly five and a half years since you past my eyes
    I look out my window and observe you — Magnificent
— In each and every way
    The little things that are taken away from you could
build a fortress one day
    Appreciate all the freedom that you have at your grasp
— Or one day you'll end up like me
      Wondering? When's the next time the moon may pass

Thoughts of a Lost Man—Gary Clarke

Reflection

    I tend to sit back and wonder why? Did they ever accept me?
    If so, then why did they neglect me? Did they ever really neglect me?
    Was I treated like the black sheep?
    As I dwell, it just might be all in my mind to me
    I entertain these thoughts and ask, Who am I to me?
    Am I a reflection of my family — Or is my family a reflection of me?
    Some say that family is not always blood deep
    True, my family acts as if they are no kin to me Father, sister, cousins, and aunts too
    Although my mother loves me and supports me no matter what I do
    God loves us regardless of what we do — He gave up his son who died for our sins
    My mom claims accepting him is what I should do — I say please forgive me of my mistakes
    I hope you love me anyways

Thoughts of a Lost Man—Gary Clarke

We're family for Christ sakes! Whether you do or you don't

I'll always remain the same — Never did Never will — Turn my back on you

That's not the way I was raised

Did I get accepted? Was I ever neglected? Does family bond ever really last?

I had the answer all along

The question should've never been asked

Thoughts of a Lost Man—Gary Clarke

Mental Battle of Self— Evolution

    Sitting still — But very active — Time moves by slowly — Life flies' bye swiftly

    Body is restricted — Spirit is conflicted — The mind tries to break free

    Although current circumstances attempts to prevent me

    Strength exudes from me passionately even when others try to distract and provoke me

    Growth — Maturity / Beautiful —Appealing   I know she wants me

    Out of fear of rejections my actions appear cocky, arrogant, cocky, she's not worthy

    Are we soulmates? Will she wait for me? Negative images begin to console me

    Pull it together - Breathe...   That was the old me Careless — Immature — Cold

    Reminiscing how she used to hold me   She's bad — I'm good Confrontation — Fight like malicious pit bulls would

    Blink — Reset — Breathe   Elevate

Thoughts of a Lost Man—Gary Clarke

Separate myself if I could　　　Epiphany — Hope my soulmate is waiting for me She's the one I need. I know now that she is the one for me

Chasing her fragrance / I know that she's close /

I pray she slows up for me

Am I to late? Can't be, it's destiny we're soulmates

Damn, what's happening to me? Who's in control of me?

Peace — Bliss — Tranquility

I see my beauty in front of me.　Drugs — Demons — Shackles

I plead to you that you are not the one for me

I let you go now perish! A better man is what I want for me

Day 2,920 still not where I want to be

Fight — or- Flight

Difficult battle is not what it should be

Thoughts of a Lost Man—Gary Clarke

A Paradoxical Freedom

Solitary thoughts — Perpetual feelings - I must succeed — At what — Failure?

I cannot

Fear stirs up delusional thoughts like if I fail to succeed then I succeed at failure

Distorted emotions disturb my psyche. Problematic scenarios penetrate my soul

Escape is the only answer, yet I can't run. Legs feels like they're plastered in cement

Backed into a corner - I need my savior. Talk to him every morning. All day every day

Well I used to

I need him he always holds me down. Empowering — Almighty — Undefeated

My safety net — Beautiful — He has no image, I am his image

In my hands we won't lose — Can I? He got me where I am now

Do I want to stay? No responsibilities — No fear — No emotions — No life

What do I do? Lost — Confused — Scared — Blind

Thoughts of a Lost Man—Gary Clarke

I can't see what's in front of me. Never saw a future. Futures doesn't come to niggas like me.

I have no destiny. Is this my destiny? Life is restricted by irrefutable dreams

More like an irrefutable reality. Am I ready?

I don't know what to be prepared for. Life is impenetrable by walls — Walls meant to suppress

Suppress Dreams — Suppress Goals — Suppress Life

Maybe the goal was to suppress — Suppress Dreams - Suppress Goals — Suppress Life

Success is protected by fear — Fear Disables Choices — Choices Limits Regrets

Yet, regrets developed while I slept

Living is possible without freedom

Freedom is possible without living

Thoughts of a Lost Man—Gary Clarke

Rotten Nooses

The collar around my neck feels laced. Manipulated knowledge leaves me
  More blue then black in the face
  Fucked up ideologies, I attempt to take the pathogen before it gets laced
  Failed attempts to be mindful that black is more than just a race — Yet — They race
  To displace — Abort missions to save face — But still
  Those strands burnt the beard off of my face. Left impressions on my neck
  Esophagus is closing — Trying to catch my breath. The forever laugh with no regrets
  Fingers pointed. Neglecting the obligatory pain that rest beyond incomprehensible deaths
  These strings strong enough to sway my body from right to left
  Abusive views and moral codes — A history vacant — Theft
  You objectify the subjects as subjective objects forgetting to inject the worldly philosophies we
    manifest

Thoughts of a Lost Man—Gary Clarke

Therefore, you take those materials and tighten the cords around our necks

Making brothers feel like niggas forgetting the origins of a nigger

But our plight doesn't differ, nah our struggle is way to similar

Killing each other is like killing ourselves. As the devil plays puppeteer to his toys

Then throws them up on the shelf. Using lines to hang men

Laughing while we adopt games like hangman. Ignorant to the truth that we are those hung men

Holding into that rope — While our feet are dangling

Attempting to break the cycle and defeat the lynch men

Realizing that my role is more than a henchman. Fumes of mildew captures my nostrils that

leaves me dazed

Bodies laid out like naive pray — That this oppression is just a phase

Thoughts of a Lost Man—Gary Clarke

Oblivious

Intelligence is blinding - Ignorance is enlightening

The fact that I can't separate from these walls is Frightening

Complacent — Unmotivated — Enigma

Despite the feeling if yearning for more

Fear suffocates my body — Penetrates my bones — Debilitates my soul

Who am I — Where am I — Lost child

Looking for hope but needing focus — Spiritual guidance?

Oblivious to the plight

Oblivion turns to confusion — Confusion permits anger — Anger manifest to rage

Rage leads to violence — Violence leaves questions — Answers

Limbo

Fallen angel — Embraced demon — Recklessness Glorified

Ridiculed by a society, Yet I'm a product of my environment

I need out — Want change — Walls are closing in - Feeling trapped begging for change

Thoughts of a Lost Man—Gary Clarke

Cries go without nurture — Abandoned — Too old to be abandoned

Too young to be abandoned — Lost child grows while the lost man is stagnant

Held hostage by the hood yet rescued by prison

Flexible more like adaptive. Lives like both are one

Are they? Aren't they? Childhood friends are there

Laughter fills the environment and smiles mask the pain

Success stories are rare and oppression is common — Poverty is normal and family is scarce

Fathers are absent — Death is a release — Release to peace

Honour Bliss Right

The only right we have

Thoughts of a Lost Man—Gary Clarke

Lost Man Forgotten Child Pt.2

I never knew that I needed you — Based upon my arrival you were never present

Yet, you and me are one and the same. Not — 2 — My reflection is evident

I didn't know that you existed but, my existence wouldn't be relevant

They put lil in front of my name s000 it's obvious that someone was bigger

At the age of five — your image in my life was fast quick like the flash from a trigger

Who the hell was I supposed to be, a boy setup to be an ill advised nigger

You placed it all on her but lil sis had conditions

Which felt like that love for me started to wither

The streets became my advisor — Teaching me not to care it would only make a man bitter

So I came up swinging / Trying to be the #1 hitter.

You pop up and I laugh Your memory drifted down some unknown river.

Grab two paddles and stroke -   Hope never allowed me to cope

Thoughts of a Lost Man—Gary Clarke

    Knowing that making it past this threshold was just a joke
    So you slid — That drip from my nose, yeah that mask cover and hid
    Emotions I couldn't decipher — Too tough but I'm just a kid
    Now I keep my eyes buried low, protected by my lid
    They say the eyes are the portal to your soul, I guess mines are as dark as the abyss
    You had another family on the side — And — Decided that I was the one to miss
    That caused a rift — Tectonic plates shift
    Embedded in my head that I'm a worthless piece of shit
    I took it out on the world — Because life is a double bladed bitch
    All I knew was my hopes and dreams never lived — Stale born — and discarded in a ditch

Thoughts of a Lost Man—Gary Clarke

Debilitating Realm

    Physically depressing — Emotionally deprived — Caged like animals and treated like slime

    A world inside a world, false realities depicted by TV

    The struggle of my comrades, it's explicit in our ability to articulate our feelings

    Words are subtle — Body language is depleted, on the outside looking in we appear defeated

    Defeated by lies — Defeated by truths

    Defeated by inescapable pain — Defeated by unfought battles

    Bellowed voices of unheard children — Down — Undignified — Out, but still in

    Land of the living dead; Forgotten: Heroes — Legends - Superstars

    Burial ground for the misunderstood, air filled with embalming fluid

    While resting on metal slabs

    Restrain the restricted and surviving seems obsolete — Came in broken yet, I'm leaving destroyed

    Disheveled — Obliterated — Damaged

    I'm motivated for better things   Yet

Thoughts of a Lost Man—Gary Clarke

Obstacles

Obstacles

Obstacles

They implement themselves in my dreams, so visions of victory. Appears like a pipedream

Needs to numb the pain therefore, brothers and sisters live off of a pipedream

Shaking and stumbling — Growling and mumbling — Speak up!!

Opportunity strikes, 1 voice doesn't matter — 2 voices it doesn't matter

Fight against oppression, others chose to do the latter

Accepted futures and defeated souls and the safe space is to

Revert back to the hole

Thoughts of a Lost Man—Gary Clarke

Grey's Anatomy

Let us pray

Boy your heads for the young boy's anatomy who's now left — Grey — Lifeless

From the obstacles that left him victim — Prey —

Difficult to articulate, how the voices in my head manipulate and send me the wrong way

But — unlike Meredith — This narrative voice is dark, all black and a little white is the plague

Gray — From these demented dreams that tormented the scenes — Where —

McDreamy couldn't dissect and connect what projects from my mental scheme

Please

Come to my aid — Resting on a metal slab — Gray — Shonda write me new scenes

Because my season is ending where black fused with white and Grey is bleeding into my dreams

Reality is

These Gray walls leaves me depressed — Because —

The pigment of my skin was there primary focus — But that silver fades to Grey

Thoughts of a Lost Man—Gary Clarke

Those chains left stains - Black embedded so deep I be damned if I expose this

Wish I had dementia like Dr. Grey, so these living memories fade — I am no longer brave

It's hard to cope — A brothers hopeless — But you are chosen — More like frozen

What melt trickles down black — That leaves you — Gray — The white feels like they're golden

But this cast is broken and not a word is spoken

All that's left is hate while the devil laughs cause we're choking — Shock his chest — He's going

Grey clouds part open

But that DNR tatted on your chest won't allow a fresh start over

The good die young — Where taught that when we're done

Painted on t-shirts — Wit black and white photos yet, you're Gray when your gone

Whether it's R.I.P or free all the homies — 4 walls are the structure of your new anatomy

New organisms organize to enhance — Recidivism —

News flash smartass we never left the prison system

Vision so Grey that destruction is the only way to make you listen

Thoughts of a Lost Man—Gary Clarke

Where you give us a tray to eat from and a pot to piss in

But your anatomy breaks down when we redraft that prescription

Then you write on your white slip — With black ink — Mass incarceration is the new prescription

Many people shifting — Paperwork is sifting — E.K.G goes flat — Grey's Anatomy

Undefined Syndrome

Thoughts of a Lost Man—Gary Clarke

Lady Insanity Sings the Rage

For my sisters I see your pain

Dolce bag, Versace skirt — These red bottoms bleeding leaves more than stains that hurt

I should've made a noose out from those blood laced panties

Instead I make them pay to see that switch under my skirt

Mutilated hymen got me skeptical of my worth

So I levitate — Stay high off of that Granddaddy Cush

Somewhat of a martyr — Because —

It reminds me of when I used to sit on Granddaddy's lap

While he whispered shush — Then he would push

Told me to keep our secret yet, there was no need to keep it

Granny would turn her head and act like she didn't peep it

Singing gospel hymns out loud in attempts to blare out my weeping

So my blessings are desecrated — Consequences from pain won't be negated

Thoughts of a Lost Man—Gary Clarke

So I torch these men to get my Zen — Laugh while they women hate it

Snatch the tracks out they hair — Snatch their breath out the air

Love it when I walk through the place and all stop and stare

Abuse them the way they abused me — Use them the way they used me

Now it's Power of the Penny or Power of the Pussy

Use social media to take the power away from those who believe they got lucky

Hashtag me too, nah Hashtag fuck you

The president gets away with abuse and you think that two words will seep through

My insanity sings the rage from the pain I've been through

Thoughts of a Lost Man—Gary Clarke

What Was

Sky blue — Light pink — Light purple
Colors so sync
Encompassed by destructible glass
My favorite one — Beautiful —
A tropical drink
Eyes water up — Reset — Blink
Surrounded by barbwire, reminiscing on memories so unique
Carefree and innocent — Didn't have to think
A drunken haze — Staggering throughout the unit
Fading in and out of their conversations — Listen
Clutching on to the old days
Remember when so and so, walked into the stop sign
Looking at what's her name
Jubilation breaks through as they speak
Grasping on to what was — Cause what is — What could
Seems so bleak
Holding on to those dreams — Cause those dreams are real

Thoughts of a Lost Man—Gary Clarke

Not living in the present — Cause these images could kill
Not living in the future — Cause this time stands still
Only living in those memories
Cause those memories you feel

Thoughts of a Lost Man—Gary Clarke

Cocoon

Self —Elevation

Delusional thoughts tempt my levitation

Einstein — Only I see the genius within the equation

But — my oppression evokes fear

So my worth only goes as far as the plantation

Self — destructive thoughts - Sheww

Stagnation

Battle within — Bad vs. Evil — Strife of the dark forces

Yet, my actions extinguished all the torches

Who am I — Analysis — Metamorphosis

Belly of the beast got me knowing that there is more than this

Or am I

That brother that loves the rep from destroying shit

Or am I

That brother who uplifts those in impoverishment

Or am I

That brother who reaps the benefit from clapping shit because I thrive from it

Yet

Thoughts of a Lost Man—Gary Clarke

Both individuals reside in the cocoon of the man that cries from this
I strive
Find the pride for the man who must survive from this
Manipulated ego denies me to hide from it

Thoughts of a Lost Man—Gary Clarke

Four Walls

Four walls

These four walls do more than restrict the body — A trespassing law for the mind

Caution tape foe time

These four walls are unbearable, yet they get more accepting with time

Breaking me down — Driving me insane — Barriers everywhere I look

I utilize these four walls to bury my pain

Coddle your emotions — Leave them in the hut

Talk to those walls — Communicate — It's fine

22 hours 9 years

My problems filled these walls with grime

These walls begin to speak — Boy you mine

Four walls start to close

What's the difference from a coffin

Forgotten Souls — Rotten Bodies — Forgotten Time

Dungeon, cave some call it a tomb

I call it the place where demons begin to loom

Quick flashes of.light illuminate their moves

Take off the head and the body is doomed

Thoughts of a Lost Man—Gary Clarke

These four walls sequester my thoughts — Dissects my mood

Infiltrate my mind — Damn — These walls start to soothe

Alleviate the distressed — Feelings began to regress

Ambitions are suppressed as the loved ones regressed

Four walls are the only requirement

To put a man to rest

Thoughts of a Lost Man—Gary Clarke

Lost Man Forgotten Child Pt.3

My tears leave scorched streams on my face

When the producer of my mind directs scenes of him being displaced

How was a child so young supposed to win the race —
When —

The main one who was supposed to show support never set the pace

His younger replication may have caused her aches

Pain from the pangs of her only son being lost without a trace — Stray —

A woman raising a man but he's a boy — Her method was attempts to coddle

So his strength was already laced — Obstacles came and he was pushed to the back

Felt like he was out of place

Think of a child caught in traffic — Because he's struggling to tie his lace

Bystanders walk by and laugh, thinking it's a game he's playing

Another black boy lost - Such a damn disgrace

Thoughts of a Lost Man—Gary Clarke

Victims of objectification and the only thing left is justification
Forgotten in a trance of
Meditation
Taking un-prescribed prescriptions of
Medications
The body is alone because the mind suffered from
Decapitation
So hopes and dreams float aimlessly
Levitation
Left with feelings of absence, suffering, depression, and desperation
Heart's open for acceptance but nobody is taking applications
Life gave him this meal meanwhile pain and tears are his only form of defecation
Too young to ask questions — Answers were never given

The balance of chaos began its dance of manipulation
So the lure of anger and hate — Seduced him — Making him weak to the temptations Now gone with the grief of the streets — Knowing that these visions aren't

Thoughts of a Lost Man—Gary Clarke

dreams Because the thoughts struck so deep that it made him weep

Thoughts of a Lost Man—Gary Clarke

First Love

Since the day you were born I knew my life would shift — My angel — Precious gift

Heavenly sent my only source of bliss

As I sift through flicks and think of memories such as this

Like when I would hold you up high and say give daddy a kiss

You would pull my hair and bite my nose, not one spot on my face did your saliva miss

But still I wish that you had more memories and none like this

Just know my love will prevail and you are eternally missed

So when you think that you're all alone and your eyes begin to twitch

Know that I'm thinking about you, every second — Without a glitch

When you cry I cry and when you hurt I scream

Happiness for you is all that I can dream

The love of my life nobody comes before you — Before chance afforded you the ability to breathe

Thoughts of a Lost Man—Gary Clarke

All I do is adore you and all this time we're apart my heart forever weeps

But I hold sacred all of our sweet memories — I love you more than I love me

This is only a pocket of time — God moves mountains — So could we

Just smile my darling — Soon we'll be complete — I'm proud of you every second, minute

52 weeks

You're the reason I open my eyes and the last thought before I fall asleep

A father's love for his daughter only grows stronger it can never grow weak

Remember my love — When you think your day is turning bleak

My heart is your heart which is as pure as God made it be

November 25th 2006 my favorite day no other can compete

That day I was blessed from above when you was given to me

Thoughts of a Lost Man—Gary Clarke

A Letter to Mom

Why do I appreciate pain when it's presented to me — Secrete this blood when I slice my vein

Give my life to those whom I love and alleviate their pain

I did horrible things in my life therefore, karma comes back in vain

Failed attempts to be noble terrified if my loved ones lay lame — Forgiveness is obsolete

There's only one to blame — For you I pray — Pray for better days

I smile, to hide the tears that drenched my bed — Body's burning from sulfur engulfed to my head

Because of you, I'll endure it a thousand times over

Wishing that God place you in his hands and allows you to sit upon his shoulders

Carry you because that's what I should've did — Joy across your face because you love your kid

Instead — Foolish - I caught this bid

Preventing you from achieving your goals I never meant to seal that lid

But now as I lay still — Seclude myself because I hate the message that was revealed

Thoughts of a Lost Man—Gary Clarke

Decoded it myself, ignorant to the fact that I caused those tears beneath the veil

Now I fail to feel, to feel what I failed — Tears cracking the pavement like golf ball sized hail

All hail be the glory if it's necessary to change the narrative of this story

Dreaming dreams for you because you deserve a better story

To I apologize and I hide my pain with smiles but I feel the hurt behind your eyes

This is my promise — One day my goals will be accomplished

You will be proud, because this jewel was never tarnished

Redefining my purpose, all I needed was a little polish

Pure love from my heart all hate shall be abolished

Thoughts of a Lost Man—Gary Clarke

A Soul that Cries

Your heart breaks as you believe mines melts away — Truth be told

The ice chips that drips from my face points the other way

It kills me to hear the pain in your face when you see the life leave my voice

Yet, the gears of my life shifted with one quick choice — So — How can I

A suffering mortal — Mere man — Be happy when I was the demise to your sacred plans

They say that love is supposed to be unconditional, but this loves has barriers

Which limits how it's reciprocal — Define the time — When I walked this imaginary line

I'll breakdown it's essence, it was an illusion of your mind

Perpetual nightmares of brothers left delusional — Too much time

I'm unable to comprehend the messages sent to my mind

Thoughts of a Lost Man—Gary Clarke

I expect your neglect — I won't regret what I can't forget

The pain of my realm suffocates the devil has his foot on my neck

Therefore I cry

These dry tears rip through my pride

A warrior sheds blood not tears — What about those who wait to die

Remove the clay from your shield and your soul begins to fry

Therefore I cry

The beat in my chest lost rhythm — Tomorrow died — Now I

Search for tactics to survive — The methods I used caused pain — Left fear Swung and I missed — Fight felt like I never tried — Beaten' to obliteration Not knowing who, what, where, or how I - I — Was involved in the altercation

Therefore I cry

Cry for the millions of eyes — Millions of lives - Millions of lies — Millions of tries

Felt like I cried millions of times - But —

My eyes, face and pillow are dry

Why?

Thoughts of a Lost Man—Gary Clarke

7 years of Deprivation

Bones clattering with anticipation — 7 long years of deprivation

Facial expressions and nonverbal cues — Reflects jubilation

11 months

She has no memories of interactions — Remnants of her father's face

Never had that satisfaction

Phone calls and visits through Plexiglas

Only images that appear when reminiscing on their past

Winks from her father as he sits at the head of the class

Soothes her mind — Maybe a hug and a kiss at last

No barriers to prevent this wish, yet too fearful to ask

Oblivious to the man that's separated from his class

Taking pictures with loved ones in his grasps

Her eyes locked onto the man separated from the class

Only sees her father — Wanting new memories because she hates the ones that she has

He moves swift and is gone in a flash

Found him, she runs

Thoughts of a Lost Man—Gary Clarke

Not knowing that she can move so fast
He grabs her and holds her tight — The whole audience gasps
Tears begin to fall — He consoles her like a father should
Wishing he'll never let go
He squeezes like he never would

Thoughts of a Lost Man—Gary Clarke

A Precious Gift

I'm forever in my mind yet my mind is frozen in time

My life flies by while I'm at rest - Still

Point of no return — No future for me, what does the world need of me

Nothing

Without me the world is in harmony

Swift changes in my life leaves me paralyzed

Inane — Incredulous - Incompatible

Hope! What is this hope?

Hope is an uncomprehendable word that people speak of

Hope is incomprehensible, a wish that will never come true

Pause... Breathe... Linger...

Faint laughter, so beautiful, so heavenly, so attractive, so angelic

Louder, so close but where, I feel blind

I hear but my vision is tampered with

Eyes clearing and laughter is getting louder

Who is this angelic music coming from? I'm searching but to no avail

Thoughts of a Lost Man—Gary Clarke

At last my vision is clear and I see my angel — So beautiful, so charming, so inspirational

Eyes alluring, conversation rejuvenating, interaction mesmerizing

My life is changing — Brighter, Optimistic, Hopeful

Hopeful? Damn hopeful — This angel gave me hope

Gave me life — Gave me hope for life

She blessed me with her laugh, her smile, her time, her hope

Heavens parted, demons darted — This angel descended from above and gave me hope

Cherish her, embrace her, thank her, never forget her

She gave me something that will last a lifetime Hope

Hope for a better life, hope to live right, hope to inspire others, hope to live

I now have hope due to my angel

My angel gave me hope

You gave me hope

Thoughts of a Lost Man—Gary Clarke

7 years of Separation

Nervous about what's to come — 7 years if separation to be undone

Shifting in his seat — Hoping that she doesn't run

New father, new adult at the age of 20

Last time he embraced his daughter — She was 11 months' young

Memories of drool dripping on his face or her sleeping while he sung

Frantic because he won't eat her soggy French fries

He participates because it hurts him when she cries

Brain now consumed with barriers, guns and badges

Inability to cradle his child — Treated like a savage

Suppressing the anger in order to show her that love is the right of passage

Looking at the clock — This ceremony is taking up too much time

He winks at his daughter — She smiles - It soothes his mind

Praying for that overdue hug and kiss

Yearning to engulf this moment — Her scent he loved is missed

Thoughts of a Lost Man—Gary Clarke

The man in front of him is taking too long and he's starting to get pissed
He hears his name, gone he moves so swift
Looking for his child — Right in front of him — Time doesn't exist
Telling her that he loves her and praying that she remembers this
They both cry from this temporary moment of bliss

Thoughts of a Lost Man—Gary Clarke

Limbo

It's hard to comprehend the sadness that comes with loss when it already appears like I already
    lost everyone
    When I am gone are they already lost
    Emotions become so frigid, my eye lashes are succumbed by frost
    Exterior appears to be hard as a shell but to the touch — Cushion — Bobopedic
    Collapses due to it being soft
    Frozen time — Leads to stagnation — Stagnation hardens all that is soft
    Comprehending the depths of depression — Means of alleviation is too far off
    To me — Lost — The lost ones always scoff
    Forgetting the existence some claim is better off
    At times I tend to agree — Why? — Because life is on a permanent pause
    Trapped underneath some burning mittens — Could be explained as the devil's paws
    Tears incinerate upon my cheek, sulfur poisons my senses because my body has no cause

Thoughts of a Lost Man—Gary Clarke

Lacking sympathetic empathy because I'm unable to empathize with sympathy

Stumbling down the corridor — An un-audible ring — Silence — Plays the symphony

No connection to the eulogy

Stages of aggravated manic depression airs on the side of morbid obesity

Suffocating from the breath of life — Because barriers are constantly impeding me

Damn! How do I decipher what's needed of me

By the time I get to some understanding — Blank slate

Everything was deleted from me

Thoughts of a Lost Man—Gary Clarke

Solitude

Isolation

Affliction is mental deterioration

Emotional separation

Only safe space

Alienation

Loneliness is comforting

Silence is soothing

Deprivation is intruding — Alluding

Alluding to confusion

Walls seems to be moving

Accepting these delusions

What some are afraid to admit

Losing

Losing to no opponent — Losing without a game

Losing all empathy — Lost the capacity to have faith

Winning — Won

Infinite depths of pain

Circumstances allows

Isolation to keep me sane

Thoughts of a Lost Man—Gary Clarke

Solitary

The sun rises and illuminates the 4 walls that encompasses my soul

This land is far less pleasant than the one Alice took when she ventured down that hole

You see, when I close my eyes is the only time I can envision goals — Then I

Wake up in a drunken haze and stumble to my exit

Only to be met by a controlled obstacle pushing back on my nose

As far as freedom goes — Lord knows

I go dumb dreaming that I was free — The pain I feel is now the pain I see

Now I'm numb because this was and is their ability — To critically — Analyze me

Now I — Fully understand scenes in a movie — Like

When I reach for the mirage featuring my loved ones, that's induced by my dehydrated emotions

That evaporated motion — Leaves no answers not a notion

Now I'm stuck in a quest wishing someone wrote in the script that healing elixir

Thoughts of a Lost Man—Gary Clarke

That eureka potion

So I'm sea sick by the waves of the dream that has me lost in the ocean

Yet, I never left the spot of an illuminated black hole — That warehouses my body

At times enslaves my mind - But time

Time is making it nearly impossible to draw up memories when everything was fine

When relationships and conversations aren't built around the sublime

When you understand the consequences — After you cross that line

Thoughts of a Lost Man—Gary Clarke

Lost Man Forgotten Child Pt.4

As the child gets older — Objectives become bolder

More frozen and emotions are colder

Daring anyone insight to knock the chip off his shoulder

Never knowing that the devil was the one who was replaying his grief — Over and Over

Injecting anger and pain — Numbing the instrument that controls his body above his shoulders

Declaration was his freedom — But — The slave masters still giving orders

Looking up for the one who can give him relief — Yet —

He can't define the symptoms of his own disorder

Can't comprehend the threshold, fear prevents wanting to discover what's beyond the border

Chaos seeps in — Unbalance causes my thoughts to be convoluted

Rage and destruction is uprooted

Manipulated goals and achievements — Polluted —

Lies and distress moves my life and anger fuels the pain

Thoughts of a Lost Man—Gary Clarke

While pain leads to rage and violence is what's intruded

Somebody must answer the reasons why I was forced — Secluded — Emotions sequestered

Same face, Same gesture

Body reverberates with anguish and contempt begins to fester

Searching for the prey to fall victim for the victim out of fear

Prey — Because the voice won't register

So I give up — No change for the hope to save up

Despair and aggression was the source to save — Bust

Lost in defiance no more love — Only lust

Fumes from corroded metal — Leaves me dazed — Poisonous Rust

Dreams in the blender, grinded down to a fine dust

The child drifts away, remnants fade with a weak gust

Thoughts of a Lost Man—Gary Clarke

I Fear No Tomorrows

I fear no tomorrows, because today is submerged with sorrow

Plagued rooted so deep your soul becomes hollow

I fear no tomorrows because yesterday started like today

Eyes blurred from the obstruction that disables my refuge and leaves me the prey

Therefore, I pray, - Pray for today so my dreams for tomorrow lead a better way.

Trapped in a cycle of confusion, feeling like Groundhog's day

Why fear a tomorrow when my debt is owed today

Failed attempts in a faith that led me astray

Now I pay for a life that was taken away

I fear no tomorrows — Never — The tears of today can't flow forever

Therefore, I navigate through today knowing that tomorrow must get better

Sifting through the past, lingering in the present in order to get to the gift of the future

I fear no tomorrows 7 I salute ya

Thoughts of a Lost Man—Gary Clarke

Beyond My Perception

Unfamiliar territory got me feeling like this can't be my reality
Self-mutilation marks from attempts to ensure my vitality
Unable to reconcile with life like... Is what this bitsss had for me
Some believe that your actions are irreparable
I tend to believe that their lies and truths are inseparable
It's unfathomable the psychological damage that we endure
Only thing that your mind is subject to is Zombies and oppression when looking out your door
How can you be claustrophobic, but feel safe buried under hells floor
When doors close, windows lock, preventing you from wanting more
Trump tweets obscenities, a rise in white supremacy yet they believe an economic rise is in store
Fuck it, monopolize the prison system, immigration and poverty increase recidivism

Thoughts of a Lost Man—Gary Clarke

White collar crimes remain ignored

Question is, who's the fool or who plays the fool

Euthanize the black man, form a kick starter for an animal that was treated cruel

Dehydrated from life's dreams of swimming in a blood filled pool

Stuck in an institutional induced coma, tears crusted on my face like drool

So I seek knowledge in aspirations to elevate my brain

Words turn into hieroglyphs, they helped me believe that I was sane

Fact is those who are free are locked away, those that are locked away believe they are free...

Fucked up mental game we engage — Insomnia accentuates the rage

Immune to the rules that constitute my peoples plague

Battered minds, shattered lives, benefits from this skit appears vague

Depictions are repulsive no matter what scale is used to gauge

Thoughts of a Lost Man—Gary Clarke

Beneath My Lenses I See Pain

They say a picture is worth a thousand words, well my lenses captures pain

Tears fall like monsoons; tri-pod needs a levee to sustain

Some say I'm coldhearted, sociopathic, a bit deranged

Yet, sob stories and visons of love fall like rain

Ridiculed by a society who only speak my name in vain

Yearning for consolation but only feeling pangs

So I snap flicks with a wish to catch fame

Floods turn to rivers that over saturate the memories in my brain

I improvise — Make a raft but it's foundation is built on lies

Slowly sinking and my savior plots on my demise

Who am I?

The reflection in the mirror is obscure to my eyes

I stood strong on my pivot — Values I never compromised

All my comrades are locked with me or they died

I receive more answers than questions asked

Thoughts of a Lost Man—Gary Clarke

In need of an intervention, I look to the sky
That blue turned to black, as if my lenses was assembled in the dark
Rapid waves collide with my ark
Optical illusions manifest — intruding — demanding to R.I.P me apart
Social anxieties despise the fight in me
Implement an irrigation system to reprise the life in me
Blink ... My pupils are the heart of Hurricane Harvey
Tears stream down my face, like the Nile is intertwined with the body
Tucked in a basket like Moses ... Drifting

Wishing that somebody finds me

Thoughts of a Lost Man—Gary Clarke

Ms. Direction

In search of guidance, I look at many opportunities that come my way

Indecisive about my path, I yearn for a place to focus and lay

I consult with Ms. Direction, her door is always open, she'll never turn me away

Although her baby father Failure is piercing thru the blinds stalking his prey

Tempted to change but her scent... Alluring, conversation is imploring me to stay

Her kids Homi, Bid, and Corpse; The home boys yeah they seen a lot of action

Every time I step in her fortress she flirts and flaunts satisfaction

Intoxication relieves my motivation; the way she pleases with ease but leaves devastation

Moving away seems impossible — I'm lost in translation

I follow her, she leads me, both have the common destination

Thoughts of a Lost Man—Gary Clarke

Thinking my therapist is wrong — Nah never gave it any contemplation

I saw her bring kings to their knees without hesitation

Yet, everybody worships her like she's the new salvation

Keeping brothers down brings her jubilation

Although she promised me a new life, fly whips a bad wife, the whole pie fuck a slice

Her beauty misleads her reputation, so honesty appears right

Going with her was too easy, I swear I never feared a fight

Taking me to the edge of the earth — coercive

It's a myth you don't really fear heights — Fly —

I went in the direction with Ms. Direction that led to misdirection

Stuck in a place with no direction

Thoughts of a Lost Man—Gary Clarke

Vent

Deprivation persist throughout my soul — Distorted illusions manipulate my obscured world

Contemplating about mistakes - Mistakes made before

Before choices — Choices — Choices given

Choices given with no right answer — No right way — No innocence

Only scrutiny. Scrutinized by a society that limited my options

Forced my decisions — Forced their decisions

Indecisive — Stagnant — Remote — Thoughts become obsessive

Redundant — Convoluted — Impossible to decipher

Illogical to who? Logical to you

Formidable to those who didn't walk in your shoes

Applicable to brothers who move like you — Outsiders can't fathom the truth

Naysayers derive rules to dispute — In capture — Dismantle — Rearrange the truth

Compromise the facts — Fact is

Facts are altered all the time — Time is distributed

Endless time — Poignant reality burns my eyes

Thoughts of a Lost Man—Gary Clarke

Humanity

Can humanity be given since humanity can be taken
I dwell in a realm where humanity is vacant
Control tactics is break em' — Mentality enslavement
Remove his spine — The devil to a god in disguise
Tempting fates every move — Abnormalities is the new tune
Dancing in a catacomb — Stacked full of fools
Lost mind, lost souls — Clutching onto hope
Through false truths forever told
There is no god in this hole
The human abyss depicts vivid transcript
Sacrificial Lambs — Benefits a hierarchy of profits
A hierarchy of prophets
Spoken word of eternal worlds — Forget your current life
The after is all yours — A better world
But a better world — It's outside of these walls
Outside if this time
Broken fragments repair — Given back to humankind
Until then
Humankind is adjacent — Humanity is replaced with

Thoughts of a Lost Man—Gary Clarke

Scum — Menace — Failure
You'll die before your free
Grief-stricken with the news
You allowed them to remove your
Humanity

Thoughts of a Lost Man—Gary Clarke

Love Outgrown

    Too cold to touch, too cold to feel yet, warm enough to be real
    Impossible to decipher the lack of emotions that ache to be revealed
    Unrecognizable to those who watched me grow in the field
    Carrying the burden of these layers that's too thick to be peeled
    Neglected emotions, an unconscious strategy
    Morbid soul — Defects of countless tragedies
    When they think of me — Perished, no second chance no trilogy
    Speak of this man, maybe in the form of a eulogy
    Perplexed from the idea that love is beyond my grasp
    Only pain and suffering remain in my clasp
    Therefore, I reject the ideology of feeling your pain — because my plight to you
    Minute — Irrelevant — Bullshit — Inane
    How could I not feel feelings, pain or love — Something so raw

Thoughts of a Lost Man—Gary Clarke

I guess when you're dead in a coffin that so called love wasn't without flaw
    Unbeknownst to you I'm here, still breathing
    But to you — I faded — Season after season
    Why should I cry for you? Please give me one good reason
    This love went un-nurtured, so it died — No bleeding
    I long for the day to reach my peak — breach the feat — sensations of cold heat
    Staggering to those who were there before my release
    Praying to any deity — mind, body, and soul united only wanting peace
    Until then my body shivers down tear soaked rivers
    Vision manipulating the mind because it all turned bitter
    Before you judge the judged I beg you take a look in the mirror
    I was up / You was down — Now I'm down and you're gone

    Message couldn't get any clearer
    This love got ushered off and you were the paul-bearer
So forgive but not forget or is it forget but don't forgive
This fire burnt out — No more warmth to give

Thoughts of a Lost Man—Gary Clarke

Lost Man Forgotten Child Pt. 5

I'm making my way now — Pain becomes numb and depression just phased out

Anger blends with rage and rage is the new wave that doesn't blaze out

Un-intelligent enough to decipher the emotions that sets the pace on this new route

Or blinded by what's red, listening to what the streets said

Can't comprehend the allure of this skewed clout

My ducts are incapable to cry — Lost in my hands like — Why?

Ball my fist and look to the sky — Wishing it would rain

But my life is stuck in an eternal drought

Every time I hear the ding — I step in the ring and swing

With every strike I lash like it's the last round in my final bought   But

My reflection in the mirror showcases a permanent pout

Is this what my life was determined to be about

Thoughts of a Lost Man—Gary Clarke

I took the steps to take charge yet, pain did not go that far

Keep running down this path and the reward is steel bars

Or a box that seals tight — Transparent like a glass jar

So I don't think — or my thoughts move so fast quick like a blink

Hopes pitch black like the drain in the sink — Bottomless

Because the goals don't go clink — Well —

They do when your trapped in the back seat and your fears begin too stink

Too young to stay in too dumb to stay out - But the stench of that fear turns to hate

That hate fuels the rage — Intoxicated because anger is what you thirst to drink

Each step with aggression — take my new outlook as a blessing

Never went to class — Hate life — So I don't care about the lesson

All I know was nothing is given — Everything is taken

So grabbing what's mine was the first phase of an unsolicited lesson

Thoughts of a Lost Man—Gary Clarke

Contemplation

I sit back and think about the decisions I made over time

Contemplating my choices like were they consciously mine

Or did I allow some mitigating circumstances to manipulate my mind

Every time I close my eyes I press play in hopes to catch the rewind — But -

I'm stuck in the present dealing with the consequences in my life because....

My actions permitted my choices to decline

So I search for the answers and didn't notice that my body's position was on recline

Tears dripping down my face while anger sets in place

Fusing with pain leads to rage ahead of the race

Yet, searching for the man who's supposed to guide me, but I barely catch remnants of his face

When I look in the mirror, I'm a spitting image — So I can't recognize myself

Damn it's such a disgrace

So I take steps to lash out

Thoughts of a Lost Man—Gary Clarke

Blinded by the reality that there is no hope left in this place

Therefore, there is no love left in this space

Only a hole for the soul because heaven is a fantasy consistently told

But hell is real because my pain and despair supplanted this realm and race

I attempt to evolve but old ways in new days make my irrationality be haste

Believing things could change — False — I don't have that time to waste

I project what I feel and not what I think

I cut the connection and abolished anything that could be used as paste

Which makes that inkling of right and wrong — Fade — Vanish without a trace

Thoughts of a Lost Man—Gary Clarke

Silence

In my world

Improbable

My thoughts are audible

Discussions of freedom, family — Questions

Am I valuable

My daughter thinks the world of me

Condemned by a biased society

My opinion here

Feels like I have no authority

Misguided perceptions

Ill advised projections

Wait

There's no room for objections

I stay silent

Move like a thread through a needle with perfection

Praying that one day it will be alright

Accepting

Thoughts of a Lost Man—Gary Clarke

Lost Time

I sit back and wonder how I — and brothers whose path that mimicked mine
    Articulate this concept that we call time
    I'm in an observation glass yet, I'm the one who studies their swag
    As they cuss, linger and laugh — Eyes steadily shift towards those three hands
    Knowing that this joyful pain won't last — Damn how sad
    The insurmountable seconds that past — Yet we act like minutes don't turn to hours
    Frustrated like shit — How long is this day gon' last
    I watch brother synchronize watches like at this time we'll make that Nacho blast
    But when that officer yells 5 minutes — Everybody gets frantic — Like
    300 is all the seconds left on earth that we have
    When I got sentenced the judge gave me — 13million 140thousand seconds, 219thousands hours
    9,125 days — 25 years — But time is something that I don't have

Thoughts of a Lost Man—Gary Clarke

When you're stuck in a cube and watch the news, like wow; Phones are talking to you now?

Times done changed while you stayed the same — 32 but still 21 — Probability high

When the times passes you bye — But yours remained — Still — Frozen — Praying

Some type of warmth melts away the pain

Bringing you back to the joy that time led astray — When happiness and life intertwined

Before you got lost in translation — Forgotten in time

Thoughts of a Lost Man—Gary Clarke

Pain

They say pain is a sensation that gets activated through your nerves

Which send signals to your brain that gages the levels of how much it hurts

Your mind tries to rationalize — the depths of your curse

You see my body is plagued so much that my spirits begin to search — Therefore —

I meditate thru my soul — Hoping to contact my ancestors wishing to find my worth

Started to feel lashes on my back — Sores on my hands — Blisters on my feet

This pain is beyond sense perception — It's embedded in my genetic code my pain rooted deep

Bruises from the shackles — From my neck to wrist — To my wrist to my feet

Tactical so my potential can never reach its peak

Have you ever asked yourself - Why is my existence based off of pain — I do

Week after week, but my quest for a logical answer gradually becomes bleak

Thoughts of a Lost Man—Gary Clarke

Solutions to these problems - I no longer wish to seek

I forgot how to swim and the tears on my bed are growing beyond face deep

My eyes are the portal to my oppression which led to my aggression

Because my demographic circumstances never taught me the value of a lesson

I'm infatuated by my pain — I begin to see my losses as blessings

Heart pumps Novocain, so my being turns numb, ignorant attempts to redefine my transgressions

Pain is beyond sensations, it's a concept that's felt — Generational — Pain transcends dimensions

Wait a minute — Attention — Before I neglect to mention

The societal void that negated the emphasis on prevention

Pain is encapsulated by this physical detention — You see

I yearn for the day when my condition has an intervention

Until I realized yearning is a stage of pain — That was inherent upon my conception

Thoughts of a Lost Man—Gary Clarke

Let's not get it twisted — This definition goes far beyond my perception

I see it in the eyes of my brothers and sisters, I am the embodiment of emotional neglection

I guess that's why these sensational thoughts gave way to a perpetual obsession

Here's my confession — They manipulated my pain into rage — Misguided by societal constructs

That scrutinized my appearance at a ripe age — But my pain was fed through my umbilical cord

Because my mother was oppressed and never figured out how to articulate that pain off her page

Now — This type of trauma is not a phase — Even though there's levels to this dilemma

Transitioning from a haze to a daze — so I'm muted to the answers of questions never raised

I kinda get it though, my genetic code is supposed to be immune to the oppressive rays

Which led to the conclusion that — I - I'm incapable of feeling pain

Needless to say that my existence is preordained — To dwell in the realm of pain

Thoughts of a Lost Man—Gary Clarke

Resenting the predicament that permits others to declare me insane

Yet, I'm resisting the inevitable because my biological manifestation is predicated off of

Pain

Thoughts of a Lost Man—Gary Clarke

Lost Man Forgotten Child Pt. 6

For the forgotten child that's trapped inside the lost man

I'll clutch your innocent fist in the palm of my hand — I promise to take you to paradise

Utopia — No place, no land

They say that our tears appear to never reach the soil, so it can't tarnish this land

But these tears fused with the body and the body can't distinguish the cries

Cries of the boy from the man

What do we do as we struggle to find peace that's wrapped up in a pain riddled plan

That anger quickly switched back to pain and the boy cries yet it sounds like the man

Think — Suffocate the cries before the eyes reveal the lies

That the forgotten child and lost man are forever intertwined

Nobody can discover what the lost man tried to disguise

Thoughts of a Lost Man—Gary Clarke

The forgotten child grieves because he feels like he's the reason that the plans could never rise

The man tries to convince the child it's alright his features are of a rough exterior

Softness won't be defined

But they both failed to realize that their tears revealed the truth of what's lost behind their pride

That the forgotten child and the lost man will never separate

Their soul is saturated with the spirit of pain so life drowned within their eyes

In the vastness of abandonment — I hide deep within the depths the corner of neglect Feels like a fist is clinched around my throat — Tightening the cords inside my neck Streams pour down my face and saturate my chest Excessively flowing from the painful images I can't forget Delirious from the delusions that I lived my life with no regrets Yet The anguish in my chest fuels my eyes And my eyes prevent my mind from getting rest There's no more lies and now I realize that my entire life I never slept

To the matriarchs that are here and the one that's gone, I love and adore you all and I hope that I made you proud

Thoughts of a Lost Man—Gary Clarke

Thoughts of a Lost Man—Gary Clarke

www.ingramcontent.com/pod-product-compliance
Lightning Source LLC
Chambersburg PA
CBHW052151070526
44585CB00017B/2064